בס"ד

This book belongs to: לה׳ הארץ ומלואה

Please read it to me!

The Very Best Book

by Dina Rosenfeld
illustrated by Vitaliy Romanenko

Hachai
PUBLISHING

In honor of the birth
of our dear Grandchildren
Chana and Rikal
May you grow to be a source of pride
to your parents and the Jewish People

Don Yoel & Malka Levy
And Great Grandmother
Thelma Levy

The Very Best Book

For Pinny and Aaron - the very best brothers of all! *D.R.*

FIRST EDITION – 1997
Copyright © 1997 by HACHAI PUBLISHING

Library of Congress Catalog Card Number: 96-78255
ISBN # 0-922613-76-1

HACHAI PUBLISHING
156 CHESTER AVENUE • BROOKLYN, NEW YORK 11218 • TELEPHONE (718) 633-0100

Printed in China

Water in buckets,
Water in puddles,
And water in raindrops
            that fall,
    but...

The water in my washing cup,
Is the very best water of all!

Coins in the meter,
Coins to buy candy,
And coins in the phone for a call,
but...

The coins that go to tzedakah,
Are the very best coins of all!

Bottles

Bottles of perfume,
Bottles of soda,
And bottles of milk for my doll,
but...

The bottle of wine for kiddush,
Is the very best bottle of all!

Boxes for presents,
Boxes for toys,
And cereal boxes so tall,
but...

The box that holds the esrog,
Is the very best box of all!

Oil for salad,
Oil for cars,
And oil to rub on me,
but...

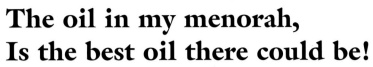

The oil in my menorah,
Is the best oil there could be!

Baskets

Baskets for bread,
Baskets on bikes,
And baskets for basketball,
but...

The basket for shalach monos,
Is the very best basket of all!

Children can run,
Children can sing,
And children can climb a tree . . .

And when we do all the mitzvos,
We're the best children we can be!

Glossary

Esrog - Citron fruit shaken together with the Lulov (palm branch) on Succos

Kiddush - Blessing over wine recited on Shabbos and Holidays

Menorah - Candelabra used on Chanukah commemorating the Menorah lit in the Holy Temple

Mitzvos - Commandments; Good deeds

Shalach Monos - (*Mishloach Monos*) A gift consisting of two types of food sent to at least one friend on Purim